Traffic Jam

written by
Leslie Harper

illustrated by
Gloria Gedeon

KAEDEN ❤ BOOKS™

The truck driver looked down the road.

He saw a long line of cars.

"What is it?" asked the truck driver.

"I can't go," said the driver in the yellow car.

"I can't go," said the driver in the blue car.

"I can't go," said the driver in the red car.

"I can't go," said the driver
of the black car.

She saw a mother and her ducklings crossing the street.

"Now I can go," said the driver in the black car.
"Now I can go," said the driver in the red car.
"Now I can go," said the driver in the blue car.
"Now I can go," said the driver in the yellow car.

"Now I can go," said the truck driver. He smiled as he drove by the mother and her ducklings.